River Dream

River Dream

Jyotirmayee Mohapatra

BLACK EAGLE BOOKS
Dublin, USA ● Bhubaneswar, Odisha

Black Eagle Books
USA address:
7464 Wisdom Lane
Dublin, OH 43016

India address:
E/312, Trident Galaxy, Kalinga Nagar,
Bhubaneswar-751003, Odisha, India

E-mail: info@blackeaglebooks.org
Website: www.blackeaglebooks.org

First International Edition Published by
Black Eagle Books, 2022

RIVER DREAM
by **Jyotirmayee Mohapatra**

Copyright © Jyotirmayee Mohapatra

All rights reserved. No part of this publication may be reproduced, stored in a retrieval system, or transmitted, in any form or by any means, electronic, mechanical, photocopying, recording or otherwise without the prior permission of the publisher.

Cover photo: Satya Patnaik
Interior Design: Ezy's Publication

ISBN- 978-1-64560-316-0 (Paperback)
Library of Congress Control Number: 2022946737

Printed in the United States of America

Acknowledgement

Writing a poem is an exciting and sublime affair but publishing them in the form of a book is an arduous task. However, it is rewarding and satisfying to see them in a book form. So, I would love to appreciate everybody who have been a part of my arduous journey.

I am immensely grateful to my revered teacher Dr. Ramachandra Behera, a renowned Odia story and novel writer, who wrote a preface to my book at a short notice despite his busy schedule. My love gushes for Dr. Aparna Mohanty, an acclaimed feminist Odia poet who has been my soul force in my poetic journey. I thank my family especially my brother Sudhiranjan Mohapatra who helped me in editing and all my Facebook friends and readers who have been my constant source of inspiration. Finally, I would like to thank my dear publisher Mr. Satya Pattanaik

Jyotirmayee Mohapatra

Preface

This is not a critique of Jyotirmayee's poems which comprise this anthology. I will rather share with the readers my impressions the poems have created in me.

I feel tempted first, to say a few words about two poems; "Gopal" and "Victory" which engaged my attention more than any other poem in the anthology did. I will try to say why.

"Gopal "is about an uncomplaining old mother, whose son takes him to Kumbha Mela, not on a pilgrimage but consign her to its massive crowd and declare her untraceable and lost. She is conscious of the intrigue of her son and daughter-in-law for whom she is now a dispensable burden. But she makes it to the Mela not on a pilgrimage as she consoles herself to have the Supreme Gopal, Sri Krishna, as her emotional and spiritual replenishment. The mother, as always, through this sacrifice, becomes resplendent and pervasive.

The world offers alternatives to cling to even when it appears to be a void with all possibilities non-existent. This sense of hope permeates most of her poems in this anthology. Jyotirmayee's anguish is evident as the spectacle of cruelty, hypocrisy, deception and rape etc. engulf values and block the path to the moral realm. This divinely ordained Mother Earth is battered and maimed by these evils, but ultimately these evils, gloom and frustration will be dissipated by the miraculous flute bringing bliss and ecstasy to the soul. This hope, I repeat, is echoed in several poems; there is an end to the present tunnel; there is always a promise of a green territory; birds chirping in gay abandon; bees collecting honey and above all, the gloom-dispelling tune of Sri Krishna's flute who is envisioned as the final saviour. Her conviction is rooted in the Indian philosophy of Time's cyclic order as hinted in the poem "River".

The second poem I have in mind is "Victory". A seed accidentally dropped in an inhospitable place, sprouts. Green stem carrying pink flower symbolises the eternal flow of life. Unafraid of hostile condition, the plant in fact registers victory of life. This reiterates the poet's perception that this world is a divine domain where good will emerge victorious.

Some of the poems are the poet's meditation as she leads a life of forced quarantine due to Covid-19. At one end such life is contrasted with the free movement of butterflies. Owing to despair, the world turns out to be godless, patients die in quarantine hospitals. The dignity of a corpse does not matter as it is distanced due to fear of the pandemic.

The despair and hardship forced upon man by this deadly epidemic are real. Man must endure it as long as it is not eliminated. On the other hand, however, as the poet looks at it, this curse is a passing phenomenon. Finally, life will remain triumphant.

Besides some of these, we may say, meditating poems, there are others based on current events which have national, racial, human and even feminist connotation. The tragedy at Galwan Valley, the murder of George Floyd by White police in Minneapolis, the death (call it murder) of a pregnant elephant that follows the fatal bombs masquerading as food and the protest of Kangana that a part of her house was demolished exemplify the above observations.

Jyotirmayee's penchant for myth is another aspect in this anthology which arrests the reader's attention. Ganga, Mist and even Taapoi etc. are given poetic treatment in the mythic perspective. Myth as a part of cultural heritage is never obsolete. It retains its relevance and enriches thoughts through ages.

The poetic statements are varied, characterised by simplicity and clarity. Jyotirmayee avoids intellectualising or philosophising her statement. Such ostentatious exercise has created enough mischief in the realm of contemporary poetry and has distanced poetry from the reader. Her poem reveals itself in an autonomous and effortless manner.

          I wish her all the best.

Ramachandra Behera

Contents

River	1
Walk	4
Gopal	6
Green Zone	8
Crazy Time	10
Quarantine	12
Covid Corpse	14
Butterflies in Prison	16
Sahada Sundari	18
Taapoi	20
Ganga Speaks	23
Vinayaki	25
Witch	27
Victim	29
Raja in 2020	31
Wall	33
Run	34
Maa	36
Bapa	38
Bou	40
In Her Eighties	42
A Dreadful Night	44
Fatal Friday Evening	46
Daddy Changed the World	48
Life is a Dream	50
A Terrorist	52
Forest Fire	53
Safety	55
Mist	56
A Green Leaf	58

Suicide	60
A Pigeon Speaks	62
The Soul Recovers	64
My Baby	65
A Friend's Illness	67
Grandfather	69
Uncage Me	72
Serendipity	74
Women	77
Mystery Spot	79
Metamorphosis	80
Medusa	82
Forest Bath	84
Dream	86
Missing	88
Victory	90

River

Always dreamt
to live in a house
on the bank of a river
so that I can see
fish playing
in river water,
enjoy sun gleaming
on their back
brightening their
silvery colour.

During rainy season
I will invite crocodiles
and they will play games
in muddy river water.

When storm will come,
big trees in my backyard
will sway to the tune of the wind,
for the birds I would surely feel sad
as they would have to leave their nests
for far and new vistas in cold.

Then spring will appear,
the smell of death and decay
will evaporate gradually
brushing the earth
with a new colour.
The sound of flute
will be heard
from behind the herd
on the green pasture.

In spring and summer,
the song of Peepal leaves
will lull me to sleep
without any workload
again, I will enjoy
the sight of rain drops
falling on river water.

Rivers have stories of their own.

Once a river in spate
in a dark night,
divided for infant Krishna
carried on his father's head,
allowing them to pass ahead.

A river is a mute witness
to the flute song,
that enchanted the hearts
of birds animals and humans,
all stood tranced along.

A river can be my friend,
can escort me to the end,
I don't wish for salvation,
I don't need glorification,
just want to enjoy life
with river forever.

Walk

Walking along
green paddy fields
submerged in
muddy brown water
stretching up to
the horizon and beyond,
paddies swaying
to the mood of the wind
clouds in the sky hiding
a weak Sun chiding,
human life lost in happy riding.

Damp smell of air
made my heart stir,
a Godless feeling
filled up my heart
with a strange loneliness
full of despair.

Surreal dreams
spread their wings,
the picture of the world
in a moment changed,
hunger clamoured,

demand for food
rose forever and ever
with rising greed and
lust for flesh
from dark caves
of human heart.

Strange to believe,
once Harappa flourished
Vedic culture survived
in a country like India
where the news of rape
of a thirteen year old,
raved and ranted
the lockdown world.

But dreams die hard
swaying with green paddies
ambling feet do not get tired.

Gopal

My son,
please don't search for me
in the huge crowd
of this Kumbha anymore.
I don't want my son
to get tired searching
for me and suffer.

You may report me missing
at the nearest police station
when you go back home
but do not put pressure
on Police to search this
old woman, your mother.

I have decided to stay alive,
joining a devotee group in Vrindavan
and spend my last days
with Gopal and I have
already received His call.

Really, I want to save you
from the embarrassment
of pushing your

old weak mother to water
and shout, "Drowning! Drowning!
save her, save her ".

Leave me in the crowd
go back home crying,
saying I lost my loving mother.
I know why you brought me
to the Kumbha on pilgrimage,
in fact I overheard Suman,
my loving daughter in law,
advising you
to get rid of me forever.
My bleeding heart pitied
your weak mind and shoulders
which cannot bear
the burden of an old mother,
and quietly I followed.

Still I love you Gopal
but for some time I forgot
that I have another Gopal,
a black boy with a flute
who will take care
of my soul
forever.

(Kumbha - a famous fair on the Ganges in India)

Green Zone

Time flows on
life goes on
there is no stopping
for vehicles,
yellow light beeps,
traffic goes on.

Humps are there
on the road
with barriers
with instructions,
road is under construction
take diversion,
orange zone.

Sometimes
one has to move slow,
sometimes
one stumbles,
falls and bleeds
then gets up and moves.
Sometimes
one faces complex phenomena
like death of butterflies

hate and greed of imperialists,
but nothing stops man
from poking at old rivalries
on high altitudes
in Ladakh.

No COVID 19
or monkey pox
can stop man
from moving ahead
surpassing the red zone.

The burnt smell
of gunpowder and blood,
reeking the air,
will be replaced by
sweet Jasmine smell,
this dark period will pass,
the azure sky will appear
with stars and Moon as usual.

The dark tunnel
will disappear,
nightmares
will end, bringing in
a green zone
with dreams galore.

Crazy Time

We met at a crazy time
when the sun was
razor sharp in the sky,
torrid heat and traffic
were singing a lullaby.
While moving on road
suddenly at red light,
all movement stopped,
time stagnated
during the traffic halt
and our hearts suddenly met.

The sparkle in our eyes
did not tell any kind of lies.

The moment was really tough.
no conversation, no confusion,
no name no introduction,
no dating not a matter to laugh
love sprouted ready
to go beyond the horizon.
Death and life did not matter,
it was not a flimsy affair.
It was more dangerous than

knowingly swallowing
burning charcoal or poison.
Knowing very well to be in love
is to remain alive in pain
and to taste death
several times,
like tasting crispy
and very hot samosa
with hot chilly fillings
or sweet dreamy feelings,
several times only
to feel pleasure
in sacrifice,
and fall in love
at a crazy time.

Quarantine

Evening saunters in,
settles comfortably
in the corners of
my quarantine room.

Door closed.

Through the window
dying sunlight
smiles outside
on the top branches
of distant palm trees
warming the hanging nests
of little sparrows
feeding their fledglings.
Night enters
through the open window
with pale cool moonlight,
spreading death like loneliness
amidst the song of night insects
and heart beats to the lilting music
of mysterious midnight.

Drenched in voluptuous darkness

and silvery cool moonlight,
suddenly the soul wakes up
from slumber and opens
its tired dreaming eyes
only to say, life from birth to death
is a long quarantine time
consisting of a few moments.

Covid Corpse

A covid corpse
moves in
a mysterious way
even though
it is just wet clay.

All white now,
whole body tied
in plastic sheets,
face covered and tied
looks like a ghost at night
accompanied by a few
from hospital in PPE kits.

Of course
how does it matter
whether it is MR Sahu or MR Mishra,
it is just a covid corpse,
one who died a lonely death
in a Covid hospital
discharged with a number tag
even the name was not to brag.

Once the corpse had
bright eyes like meteors,
his eyes blinked
like wistful stars,
his children were his passion
his family was his obsession
now he lies still and forgotten
tears cannot bring back to life
the same body once was ready
to face all strife.

It is just a covid corpse,
so, how does it matter
whether it is in a wooden coffin
or shrouded in red, white sheet
dragged to the riverbank,
when the villagers deny
six feet ground in a graveyard
or four shoulders to carry
him onto ward.

Is Covid so powerful
to deny the dignity
of a man in death
or an eye opener to truth ?

Butterflies in Prison

My butterflies are in prison
since lockdown due to pandemic,
inside the net of
four walls of the house
they fly and flutter
and silently suffer.

How beautiful they are!

Nature has painted their wings
with vibrant colours,
yellow, blue, orange and ash
drinking nectars from flowers
they sit for a while on soft petals
before spreading wings for new flowers.

Spring came,
flowers bloomed
birds twittered
gaunt trees
bore green
but butterflies
in prison
pined for freedom
pined for flowers

beating tired wings
against windows,
of course, they are kept
in prison for safety reasons.

The butterflies look at
the lawns, trees and flowers
through the glass windows
but cannot breath in fresh air,
their feet do not touch leaves,
some rare butterflies
cannot drink turtle tear
imprisoned for a long time
away from Nature.

Mind affected in prison,
butterflies fail to respond to season.
They feel like caged birds
who never sing full throated melodies,
when the heart is stifled,
mind anxious and stressed
their throats are choked.

My little butterflies
will survive this iced burning time,
one day the little ones
will understand the pandemic
and be wiser.

They will learn
not to trample with Nature
so that they can live
a life of peaceful coexistence
and avoid all disasters.

Sahada Sundari

I don't want to be
a Sahada Sundari,
live an alien dark life
among the foliage
in the hollow
of a Sahada tree.
I don't want
to come down
at midnight
to take bath in the river
do all household chores
and disappear into
the tree before sunrise.

I love to see sunrise,
love to stretch my limbs
in blazing liquid golden sun,
soak the warmth of life
enjoy life as it is.

A day may come
when a prince will arrive
from an unknown
country faraway

following my long hair
floating on river water,
and rescue me
to give me a life
of sunshine.
I always hated
to live in a palace
as the story described.
I can't live
in a Sahada tree now
as those trees
have become scarce.
Sahada trees, once
planted to prevent
thunderstorms are not
planted anymore.
Forests disappearing,
industries expanding,
Sahada Sundaries
have to wake up
at sunrise
overcoming all fear
in the morning air.

(NB Based on an Odia myth Sahada Sundari)

Taapoi

The youngest
and only daughter
of a merchant family,
born as beautiful as a lily.

Seven elder brothers
surrounded you like stars,
you were the only doll
all of them yearned to lull.

Born with a silver spoon in mouth
you became the Brahmin widow's eyesore
who made fun of you and coaxed you
to get a silver moon from your mother
and a golden winnow from your father.

Mother died before completion
of a silver moon,
father died after presenting you
the silver moon,
an innocent pampered girl
that you are,
grew up playing happily,
unaware of the dangers
lurking around you in spheres.

When seven brothers
unfurled their ships
on the blue ocean,
they promised to
bring back gifts for you
and return very soon.
Leaving you
in care of seven sisters in law
they left home happily for distant islands
Java, Sumatra and Borneo.

Again, appeared the Brahmin widow
one morning,
to instigate the sisters in law
to torture you
as the cunning woman
always envied you.

You fell from grace
of your sisters in law
who envied you long before
except the youngest one
as she doted on you.

Scanty leftover food,
bed on floor, clothes torn,
grazing goats in forest,
bearing harsh winter
in ragged attire
was your daily affair.

The trees in the forest,
the bovine you grazed,

the valley and the river
became your friends forever
but you never complained
never rebelled but patiently waited
worshipping a tribal goddess
for your brothers safe return.

Came the long-awaited day
your brothers returned from trade
sisters in law were punished
one by one their noses were cut
and you were rescued.
Maa Mangala puja by maidens
was started from that day
for the well-being of brothers.

But do you know Taapoi
you made a mistake,
the mythical slur on sisters
and sister-in-law relationship
was created for your sake.
You should have fought bravely
against your sisters in law
so, their noses would not
have been cut.

Maidens like you
should learn to fight well
to live well on this Earth
as the victory lies only
in your own strength.

(Based on a popular Odia folk tale about a maiden Taapoi)

Ganga Speaks

I am Ganga,
the darling daughter of King Himavat,
Gangotri is my parental name,
clad in all white, sitting on Makar (half
crocodile half fish)
I dreamed of being a great sojourner.

I don't remember
when I left my hometown,
with all force I swirled down,
but Lord Shiva's matted lock
made my force gentle, I learnt
to love and my mind calmed down.

Then I followed King Bhagirathi
to give salvation to his ancestors
sixty thousand of King Sagar's sons,
saved them from sage Kapil's curse.
I wash the sins of those who come to me
never distinguish between a king and beggar.

My journey continued from
Pancha Prayag to Triveni Sangam
with sisters Yamuna and Saraswati together

watched the glittering Kumbha every three year,
every day in the early mornings,
sacred chants on my bank, filled the air.
Once a young untamed maiden I was,
became Mother Ganga and accepted
offers of lighted Diyas and flowers,
and remained busy in washing sins
of kings and fakirs.

I danced to the Bay of Bengal,
watching the raucous noises
of human activities on my banks,
suddenly the Corona pandemic
made the world quiet,
and made me thoughtful.
Now it seems to me
as if time has come
for multitude of humanity
to adopt a way of life
that is simple and beautiful,
beyond jealousy and ambition,
adding love to make life graceful.

I am really tired of washing sins
for centuries and centuries.
I feel free now that
I am not a goddess anymore,
Rather a river of fresh water.
I too wish to breathe clean air
and travel far....

Vinayaki

I am Vinayaki
speaking from Mannarkkad
in the silent valley of Kerala.
A few days ago, I came here
leaving my decomposed body
in Velliyur river, after eating
pineapple stuffed with firecracker,
probably set to ward off a wild boar.

But tell me, tell me
how can an innocent
pregnant elephant
suffering from hunger,
understand that man
is a great trickster?
Of course, I had seen
much before,
many of my fraternity
chained in temples
live a dreadful life
of torture and despair.

I am now too sad
because even after my death

men don't realise that
they encroach my habitat
and a perennial war is going on
between man and elephant.
The news never mentions
about my unborn baby
who never got a chance
to see the light of the world,
and my dream of being
a mother got spoiled.

People try to give my death
a communal colour
but how do I care
whether my killer
was Wilson, Azimuth
or even Amar,
when dream of being a mother
got crushed forever.

Witch

In my village
a witch lived
in a banyan tree
who always loved
a new bride.
When the pretty bride
walked near the tree
the witch came to her
and took the bride for a ride.

Throwing off the veil at home
the bride laughed and talked aloud,
sometimes like a shy maiden she giggled.
Then the real show started
a tantric was called
who gave resin smoke to the bride,
the bride was beaten and branded
just to drive the witch out.
The bride had to carry a brass pot
filled with water
to the threshold of the door
where she swooned and the witch left.

The wizard said
the bride's stars
at birth were afflicted
with power to
attract witches at hand
so, inform her husband
to take his stand.
But neither the wizard, nor the bride's
in laws or even her parents considered
the absence of the bride's husband
who works in a distant city,
his thought might have
affected her mind instead!

During those days
nobody could understand
the witch was just a projection
of the bride's unfulfilled passion,
the new bride was lonely at heart
what she needed most
was loving care of her husband,
not a tantric or a wizard.

Victim

When a girl dies
a rape victim she is,
the first question arises
whether she cooperated
in the act and bears
all responsibilities.
Either she had an affair
with the accused boy
or she provoked him
by her dress or manners.
Sometimes the call records
are counted, nobody considers
who called whom and why,
and what for were the calls.
Nobody smells a foul play
when the girl was called,
dragged and strangulated
as the incident needs a witness.

The court and justice
stand firm on laws,
as the Mother Earth,
who was the only witness
cannot come to the witness box.

The benches sit for years,
the lawyers argue for years,
public memory fades,
the victim, silently suffers.
But the question that hurts
does the Mother Earth
give birth to girls
only to be served
as pieces of red meat?

Raja in 2020

Raja
the festival of maidens and swings
comes every year riding
the chariot of monsoon clouds,
though this year it came
drawn by swift dark corona horses.

Fear of death
hung heavy in the gloomy atmosphere
peeling laughter of maidens
sitting on bamboo swings
in Mango orchards and
music of anklets and bangles
all drowned under
the pall of lockdown blanket
brought the picture
of a bleak landscape.

But Raja in Covid pandemic time
came in a virtual world,
new clothes and jewellery
on virtual trial sold
Podapitha, Kakara, Arisa (names of popular
Odisha cakes)

by 'Pitha on Wheels 'delivered,
on online order Mangoes, Pineapples
Lychees and Jackfruits
entered the threshold.

Picture of maidens on swings
singing Raja swing songs and
'Happy Raja' messages came
in virtual world,
instead of playing cards
people interacted in social media
or played Chess
in a clean interface.

Corona was pushed to the fence
and was asked to wait there
until the rendezvous of Man
with Life was over.

(Raja - an Odia festival that celebrates
fertility of the Earth.)

Wall

A wall is always ambiguous
depending on your stance,
your choice of a place
from where you look at its presence.
If you stand on the terrace of your house,
the wall simply protects your garden,
plants and flowers, birds sitting on boughs.
If you look at the wall from the port,
where ships float and the sea sleeps calm,
it simply blocks your vision of the garden,
the beauty and the charm,
appears as a lifeless composition of grey stones.

Life is like a wall,
shrouding mysteries,
invites you to take different stances,
offers a kaleidoscopic vision
during smooth times,
teaches a lot when time changes,
gives a rough ride during a pandemic,
but says it all depends on the stance.

Run

Run, run
as swiftly as you can,
run like Atlanta
run like Artemis
run fast, win laurels
however fast you may run
remember the end is one.

Busy in running
you forgot
to think about
the meaning
of your own life.

You forgot that
the earth and the plants
the sky and water
the animals and birds
even the Sun and the stars
all have a divine presence
in them, and the same divinity
runs in man.

So, stop for a while
and remember
prize, fame and power
earned through running
cannot accompany one
after the end point
of competition
or even after Russia
and Ukraine war.

You must remember
man needs only
six feet land
in the grass lap of
Mother Earth
by the quiet river
where air is free
sunshine is free
moonlight is free
where life's
complications
remain at bay
forever.

Maa

It is so painful to remember
your fingers holding my palm
saying you don't want
to leave me and this world
forever.

How can I forget
your trembling fingers
that soft gentle touch
that   pleading look in your eyes....
could I request blind Death
to forget you, it was
beyond my power.

Your quivering lips
wanted to say many things,
but time was short and sudden
deaf Death did not give long signal
in any incurable disease,
it gave just hourly beeps.

Do you know
our home is drowned
in burial ground silence

as your near and dear ones
are not coming in this Covid time
to see your flesh and bone body
burning on funeral pyre
I am alone with my bleeding heart
to attend the world's show
where tear and laughter ends.

Sleep in peace
beyond all desires,
my loving Maa,
in God's grace.

Bapa

Long back
you added wings to my mind
probably asked me to fly in the sky
that I could not understand.

During rainy days
while floating paper boats
in flowing red water
dripping from thatched roofs
I dreamed rowing slowly
to strange far countries
which came true
after you left forever.
I remember falling down
several times on slippery mud courtyard
in the centre of our large house
you calling me unstable feet
out of affection.
You were the umbrella
that protected me from
rain and sunshine
how simple was life then!

Now I know the meaning of flying for fun
understand the meaning of greed,
jealousy, ambition and competition.

Able to walk steadily
on the same slippery ground,
you taught me how to walk on
the complex road of life
that has made all the difference.

Bou

You will be
always with me
with a ray of
dazzling smile
on your lips,
dyed with beetle leaves
instead of lipsticks.
Your bespectacled
calm big eyes
radiating with
love for life
concentrating on
knitting needles and
your deft fingers busy
with colourful yarn
was a sight to see.

I remember
your voice over phone
reminding me,
calling me if
I was late or busy
in work forever.

Now I listen to
your voice in the air
calling me sometimes
from very far,
suddenly I start
only to find emptiness near.

The zest and love for life
that I received from you
is my treasure,
I will preserve it in
my heart forever
and forever.

In Her Eighties
(In memory of my friend Sanjukta Das's mother)

When she was alive
in her eighties,
she was fondly
cherished by a few
though it was not
really her due
because she served many
during her hey days,
of course never hoped
to get help in May days.

A bundle of flesh and blood
now she lies in bed,
attended by a nurse hired,
with a pale smile she said,
life's rules are really weird,
like Sisyphus we live a life
and call it human spirit undefeated.
Ruminating past with watery eyes
she remembers her happy maiden hood,
and narrates how she came
from Bhubaneswar to Kendrapara
by boat as a blushing bride.

Without any grudges,
she lives a skylark life
blessing all and waiting for
the last moment of life.

Good for good
and bad for bad
is not the way
of the world.
So, no wonder
she never
received the love
that she showered
but she has undaunted
faith in God
and she lives
happily like a bird.

A Dreadful Night

A brutal clash
at Galwan valley
in Ladakh.

On one side disciplined Indian boys
defend LOC constantly striving,
on the other blood thirsty Red Army
surreptitiously planning
to devour everything.

Stealthily and silently
the dragons march forward
with lethal weapons
like stones and rocks
wrapped in barbed wires,
and wooden logs studded with nails,
attack breaking all war norms
more barbarous than
the Stone Age wars.

Our young boys
fight back
to protect our
velvety sleep and dreams
sacrificing their own lives.

India bows its head
in sad farewell
put wreathes
on their cold bodies
love gushes from
the hearts of millions
while the Himalaya
and Galway River
stand silent spectators.
But the Dragon
must remember,
Galwan valley
is not South China Sea
to reign forever
creating terror.

Fatal Friday Evening

Once the pilot won
the sword of honour,
he promised
to carry people home
stranded abroad in Arab countries
to God's own country,
green Kozhikode, in Kerala.

People boarded
the repatriate flight
Air India Express.
A full flight
a cool evening
but suddenly
the sky changed,
dark clouds arrived,
the pilot steered
towards Kozhikode.

At Kozhikode Calicut
International Airport,
lashing rain, slippery
ground,runway filled
with rising rain water,

poor light without ground arrester,
invited the final disaster.
The plane broke into two pieces
but the pilot sacrificed his own life
to save the passenger's dreams.

Now who can stop his old mother's tear,
who can pacify the CO-pilot's pregnant wife,
whose dreams are shattered
as her unborn baby would
grow up in a world
without the love
and protection of a father?
Can the fatal Friday answer?

Daddy Changed the World

"Daddy changed the world."
"Daddy changed the world ",
says Gianna Floyd,
six-year-old innocent
daughter of George Floyd.

The protest march on
the busy road of Minneapolis,
slogan, interviews,
mama's tear and racial injustice,
the rage against subtle social disparity
the angst of being black in white society
the death of her father and black frustration
all beyond little Gianna's comprehension.

She is not yet told
how her daddy wreathed in pain
for more than eight minutes
and several times said, "I can't breathe,"
the white police silently watched
and shot the gun instead.
Now the little girl says, "I miss my daddy
with whom shall I play?"

Is there an answer to her question?
Does the white world understand,
be it white or black, fatherly love
is the same for every child.
Will the girl be the same Gianna Floyd,
when she will grow up knowing
the truth about her father George Floyd?

Life is a Dream

Life seems
to be a dream at one point,
when you sit looking
at your heart.
A moment comes
when all memories
and all experiences
start moving in a vortex,
all melt at one point
only to find that
life's incidents
pass before you
dreamlike in a queue.
Sometimes the past
shows like present,
in the next moment
the present becomes past.
All of us walking together
on life's winding stairs
some we remember
some forgotten some bitter
and some sweet days
in our mind flutter
like the wings of

a butterfly in the sun.
Life's ambitions and desires
whether fulfilled or not
all dreamlike pass one by one
in rainbow coloured
pageants, before
the life's sun is down.

A Terrorist

Walking alone
in the multitude
in a stressful mood,
not knowing where to turn,
confused and frustrated,
stopping at red signals of life
and walking again
when the signal turns green,
pained and bored
with a blank head,
the young man
looks ahead.

Suddenly a soft hand
drags his hand,
entices his heart
to a dark and violent
death valley,
in the name of rosy heaven
in the name of religion.
A terrorist is born
who lives on gunpowder,
kills thousands
transforming green earth
to blood red colour.

Forest Fire

Forest is burning
for days together,
wild animals running
halter-skelter like
trees shedding leaves
before the arrival of winter.
Mother Nature shocked,
stands aloof, dumb and confused.
Her eyes are dry
trying to cope with the pain
like a mother waiting
outside the ICU
with a vain hope
of her child's well-being.

The sky is crying blood,
it spits volcanic heat
with sleepless red eyes
reflecting forest fire.

The night is pained
crying aloud
in hissing hot air,
stars are red

the moon is red,
where is love!!
love hides
in poet's heart and pain
to emerge after the fire.

But mankind sleeps
enjoying deep sleep
unaware and careless
about the effect forest fire,
when destruction of forests
invoking annihilating forces,
indicating a doomed future.

Safety

Heavy rain cannot drown
burnt smell in the air,
sparkling rainwater cannot silence
the cry of corona patients
running here and there,
when a covid hospital is on fire.

Crazy and panicked
firemen carry dying patients,
oxygen tubes hanging,
relatives carry cylinders
into ambulances,
and the evening is smeared
with frustration and unhappiness.

The moon cries with stars
hidden behind clouds for hospitals
running without fire safety certificates.

Foul   politics plays chess
with innocent lives,
when the king and queen
enjoy the evening,
with steaming hot tea,
music and dance
non -stop streaming.

Mist

In a mystic land
that is India
mist was created once
by the great sage Parasar,
when one summer,
smitten by love, Parasar
fell for fish maiden Satyavati,
the princess of a fisher king
while she was ferrying
a boat across the Yamuna River.

He promised her a talented son
who would write epic of a nation (India),
but the maiden Matsyagandha
famed for her foul smell
and irresistible beauty
was scared of
the sage's dark complexion
and the physical union
with him under the sky open.

So, the great sage Parasar
exercising his mystic power

covered the place with fog
and by his mystic power
the fisher maiden's body's odour
was changed to sweet smelling flower.
The dark-complexioned boy
Krishnadwaipayan Vyas was born
out of that union,
destined to write
the epic Mahabharata .
The history of
the great Kuru Pandav war
was lying hidden
in the womb of Satyavati
for a long time
along with her ambition.

*(Based on the myth of birth of Kuru and Pandav
dynasty in the epic The Mahabharata)*

A Green Leaf

Who knows
why a green leaf
silently fell down
long before
it turned yellow
long before
the arrival of Autumn.

The onlookers
said many things,
the leaf was too weak
so, like a shooting star
unable to stick to the sky
it was born to die early.

Some said
an incurable
disease like cancer
had worn its stem,
some said,
the wind loved
to caress it.

The green leaf
did not try
to understand
the mystery of
cruel destiny,
or the mystery of
nature, life and death,
rather it turned brown
among other fallen leaves
became a part of dust
slowly and slowly.

The onlookers
silently looked on
shedding tears
but failed to know
why the leaf fell down
so early before it matured
and failed to understand
why the Sun is indifferent
and why the Sun shines so brightly
even after the leaf
fell down untimely.

Suicide

Today she called me over phone
to pour her heart out
about her snake like selfish children,
and leech like greedy kinsmen.
She said, at seventy-five,
she has lost all stamina,
all mental strength
to fight the war of life.

She has already packed her trunk
with medicines and pension papers
ready to leave for a life lonely and greener,
where nobody would chastise her
for past incidents or goad her
for money or some favour,
or else she would jump into a river
to end the life with so many problems
is not a great matter for her.

Shocked and sad,
quietly I told her
try to perceive life
as a beautiful flower,
enjoy the beauty of sunshine,

the golden sunset,
the moon and the star,
laugh more, listen to the birds
singing there and open your heart
to the sorrow of others
don't strike a blow to the sail
of your own boat to sail quickly,
wait for a natural gust of wind
which will take your boat to the shore.

A Pigeon Speaks

I am a pigeon.
people love me
as a bird of good omen,
entertaining and enjoying
singing throaty coos often,
strutting and inflating plumes
on the walls of the temples,
I enjoy my life where
once the stone dancers
danced in the moon and sun.

I love to be with people,
carry messages of peace and love,
lovers enjoy my company
as night enjoys
the fragrance of jasmine
my great sense of direction
helps me to fly back home,
but hate and war changed my role,
from love birds
I became messenger pigeons for sure.
My cool life of complacency
gave way to the job of a messenger.

When I was caught near the sea
with rings on my claws and toe
with messages in unknown language,
I was really pained …
Could anyone imagine,
a poor pigeon's agony....

The Soul Recovers

For a long time
lost in the steep terrain
of emotions and dreams
suffering from dejected moods
of gloomy dark nights
the soul is recovering slowly,
opening its tired eyes
to bath in the morning Sun
gliding slowly to the sky
spreading splendours
on rain lashed paddy fields
to remind heartbroken peasants
of moon blanched harvest nights.
The soul feels the splendour
and starts to sing a new song
of Janus-faced time.

My Baby

My baby opens his eyes
when hospital beds are filled up,
countries are in lock up,
Wuhan to Antarctica
is not far to travel
but hospital beds
are not available
as if the old Earth
needed to shape up.

Roads empty,
airfields empty,
coffee shops feel lonely,
Gods die a natural death
temple, mosques
and churches closed,
may be forever with loss of faith
but apples fall on the Earth
and quiet flows the river.

Sea waves whisper and kiss
the lonely and deserted beach
lost in love song and ecstasy
shadowless giants take strides

to avenge on greedy man
who destroyed Nature's beauties.

My baby cries for the first time
after trying hard to leave the womb
cries of hunger pierce the air
when I try to open my eyelids
loaded with tiredness of ages
I Listen carefully,
a voice streams in and says
a baby can be fed in all condition
by nursing mothers.

My baby's eyes twinkle
like a lone star in the west
in the evening sky,
my baby's time starts
from this moment on the
arid, dream burnt planet.
So, I pick up the baby
to give him protection
from the dark sunset.

A Friend's Illness

A friend's illness
certainly
makes me sad,
shocks me, jolts me,
probably keeps me
on my guard.

Sleeping and languishing,
listening to Death's silent arrival,
in a swift swishing airplane,
smiling friendly Death sitting
in pilot's cockpit, ready to lull
the plane moving towards sun rise,
blue white clouds underneath
rivers, green paddy fields
hills, deserts and fountains,
vistas from airplane's window
is certainly life's call.

It does not feel good
to sympathise one
with the same fate,
sitting together
in the same boat

on a turbulent ocean
with a tiger inside
like Life of Pi,
the same story
of struggle and victory
and defeat at venue
add salt to life's menu
and is repeated again.

So, let's celebrate life
to the last moment
and be empathetic
rather than be pathetic.

Grandfather

When Durga Puja came every year
with a mild touch of cold in air
and festivities in atmosphere,
grandfather arrived
with story books galore.

He opened my window
to the fantasy world
where snakes and witches
in darkness lie curled,
stories of Ten Princess,
the Arabian Nights tales
Chakulia Panda Odia folk tale
and many more stories poured on.

Starry eyed we listened
with rapt attention.
 I listened to stories,
sitting like a stone in fear,
how the old witch
stole the baby princess
and the princess grew up
to be a beautiful maiden.
To rescue her,

a prince arrived from a distant land,
but seeing him
the skulls on the wall laughed
and the witch was killed
by the prince.

Sometimes I travelled
with the stories,
on a narrow path,
in a dark jungle
leading to a tiger
that came to eat Indian pancakes
offered by an orphan brother and sister.
I shivered in fear
at his realistic narration
and was transported to
a wonderful world of illusion.

Both of us went to the library together
he always said a library is more
precious than all the riches forever.
The books in the library
contain all knowledge
that come to your rescue
whenever necessary.
I fell in love with library
and started a personal one
which provided me relief
from life's mess up and
all confusion.

Library provides knowledge
and varieties of experience,

helps to find essence
of existence through books,
man does not feel hurt
even if he trips and falls.
Thus, library is a lifelong companion
more dear than any other person,
this knowledge is certainly
grandfather's contribution.

Uncage Me

Come,
uncage me
from this diamond -studded cage
from the fountains of desire,
from the golden fruits of attachment of love
and make me free
from the dream of a distant island
where I eat lotus and drink honey
among yellow flowers, butterflies
and dance to the tune of music
of life like many others.
Everything is dead
now around me,
even the vultures die
rivers lose their tracks,
heat rises, trees vanish
distant blue hills are not
attractive or mysterious
wolves have no place
to hide in the forest
but I am a prey of
of my own desire.

How can one live
in such a dreary desert
so, come, it's high time
to make me free O God
if you don't come
I will break all shackles
to fly up and beyond the horizon
of dark desire
and see your blue eyes
having power to
convert death to nectar.

Serendipity

When dark clouds
gather in the sky,
light gives way
to darkness,
life becomes
a long dark road
without a dawn
without the Sun
without a glimmer
of light for long,
it becomes difficult
to take a step
and all movements
are suspended,
life becomes
lonely and unbearable
direction is not known,
there is only rain
and lashing rain
with lightening
as a companion.

A miracle happens
at that time
to dissipate all darkness.

O beautiful Lord!
You appear
in the distant horizon
playing on your flute
enticing all lives
breaking all
silences and loneliness .
Your blue eyes
penetrate into the heart
of the lost travellers,
You call them home.
The lilting music
from your flute
dissolve all gloom
provides warmth and
comfort to the soul
and the soul starts to sing.
Sleepy birds sitting
among the leaves
suddenly start singing,
rainbows appear
in the rain-washed sky,
sea waves beating
their heads on sand
carry surf flowers
to the shore.
The flute song
continues on and on
making life a celebration.

Suffering, death and darkness
disappear in your grace,
love cascades vigoursly

drowned in love's ecstasy
the lost traveller's heart
dances to the rhythm
of your flute's call,
you are the magician of eternity
creator of wonderful serendipity.

Women

Loud women
are not human beings,
logical women
are not living beings
or loving beings !

A woman should be
coy and bashful,
with curves of body
that is lustful,
selling beauty
for gain in consumerism,
is now said to have humanism.
But when a woman
is intelligent and fearless,
moreover if she has talent,
then she has to be
chastised in open court
like Gargi by Yajnavalkya
and has to remain silent.

Now Kangana is not silent,
she is intelligent,
fearless and has got talent.

When many were cool,
why did she pull ?
Did she commit a mistake
by putting her life at stake ?
She is Manikarnika,
and has the gaze of Sita.
She is a woman
who defies male domination,
she knows that
she lives in a place
where Dawood's
house is still safe,
but she is just a waif.

Women can defeat
the insecure demon,
and prove that
enough human values
still left on this planet
to live on with a sonnet.

Mystery Spot

Winding uphill
through tall Redwood,
Oak, Eucalyptus trees,
and hairpin bends,
experience Nature
in her best attire,
you come to Mystery Spot
in Santa Cruz
to discover,
law of gravity
defied forever !!
Fascinating, exciting,
a trick of perception,
engineered in a slanted room
at twenty degree angle
inside the tilted house,
that creates visual illusion,
may be in the absence
of a horizon.

Metamorphosis

My grand daughter
fluttering like a butterfly
on terrace garden
became a caterpillar,
one day only at the age of eleven.
She did not understand
the meaning of this change,
the fears, burdens and strife
of this transformation in a girl's life.
She did not know
that Nature has made her
more powerful than other beings.

A butterfly knows no anxiety,
visiting flowers is only its piety,
it has to become a pupa or chrysalis,
liquid state from which a butterfly
emerges again after pumping blood
into its colourful wings.
But my butterfly just entered into
a period of stress and depression,
her mind still a butterfly roaming
in the forest of imagination,
but her body a caterpillar,

tied to the world of convention.
A strange juxtaposition
which she has to balance,
and again flutter like a butterfly
among the flowers on terrace.

Medusa

Medusa,
ravishingly beautiful Medusa,
one of the Gorgon sisters,
known for her snake black lock
which later turned to snake looks
that turned the one who looked
at her to stone.
Punished by Athena
for having relationship
with Poseidon
before her marriage,
she was destined to give birth to
noble winged Pegasus.

Her eyes were greener than the
sea Aegean,
lips more red than rose
in Parthenon.
Born to be a priest in Athena temple,
Medusa became cursed
because she boasted
about her beauty and fell
a prey to Poseidon's dirty deed.

While guarding the Aegean Sea,
she was killed by Perseus
by looking at her reflection in a shield
and her head adorned Athena's sword.
But self-centred bragging Medusa
was in search of happiness,
which she probably got
by being placed as
Athena's aegis.

Forest Bath

Tall trees in the forest
lure and call every day,
mysterious and delightful
as red Gulmohars in May.
How to resist them,
how to keep them at bay ?

Boxed city life in apartment
sucks life spirit from heart.
So, embracing, feeling and
smelling trees at sunrise
that seem to touch the sky
and enjoying fading star flowers
studded in the blue canopy,
absorbing all sounds, and
calming smell of morning forest,
heals the wounds of the heart.

Slow meditative stroll on
quiet, narrow forest roads
where sunlight streaks
through tall trees,
is true forest bath that
gives tranquility and peace

to heart and mind.
Forest bath is beautiful
and spiritual, that connects
God to individual.

Dream

He intrudes my dream
every night
several times,
and disappears
when I open my eyes.

He comes
with peeling laughter,
his innocent eyes
and loud voice
say a lot,
but words fade
into oblivion
when dream is broken.
Memory fails to prison
his physical features
except his liquid eyes.
Who is he ???
Baby Krishna
or an angel !!!

Dream breaks
like a cracked glass,
pieces fall on bed,

eyes grope in darkness,
someone laments in sleep,
baby Krishna stops crying.

Sorrows are buried
on this brightly lit earth,
hearts never burst
when a new sun rises,
love permeates between
dream and awakening
dream turns to illumination.

Missing

God is missing,
God is missing,
since how long
nobody knows.
Probable time
may be,
when the waves
were whispering aloud
words of love,
stars were dreaming
on blue sky bed,
the sun and moon
both were waiting in the
distant orange horizon
to come ahead,
a pandemic was
spreading its
hungry wings
to devour the world,
God left home.

Who knows
where did He go,
may be to blue unknown

where He can create
a new fresh world ,
envy free, COVID free
and competition free,
love gushing everywhere.

Flowers are still blooming
in God's garden
falling down on the ground,
nobody plucks them anymore,
to make garlands to deck God.

God's home is dark
until He comes back,
an FIR has been lodged
to find the missing God.
Can human Police trace Him
if He does not wish
to come back to this
confused world.

Victory

When a green stem
carrying a pink flower
comes up cracking
the hard asphalt road,
without nurture,
without care,
we can call it
survival in nature.

The seed that sprouted
might have been carried
by a squirrel or air
or a vehicle carrying
sacks of seeds
must have dropped
the seed on the road.

The seed sprouted,
grew up, breathed,
swaying in the wind
from side to side
declared that
life will survive
even in unfriendly condition.

Black Eagle Books

www.blackeaglebooks.org
info@blackeaglebooks.org

Black Eagle Books, an independent publisher, was founded as a nonprofit organization in April, 2019. It is our mission to connect and engage the Indian diaspora and the world at large with the best of works of world literature published on a collaborative platform, with special emphasis on foregrounding Contemporary Classics and New Writing.

www.ingramcontent.com/pod-product-compliance
Lightning Source LLC
Chambersburg PA
CBHW030232100526
44583CB00013BA/967